THE MODELS BOOK

By ANNIE OWEN
Written and Edited by Claire Watts
Photography by Jon Barnes

CONTENTS

page	2-3	Equipment
page	4-5	Play Dough I
page	6-7	Play Dough II
page	8-9	Marzipan
page	10-11	Salt Dough
page	12-13	Oven-baked Clay I
page	14-15	Oven-baked Clay II
page	16-17	Soft Clay
page	18-19	Cake I
page	20-21	Cake II
page	22-23	Clay I
page	24-25	Clay II
page	26-27	Papier Mâché I
page	28-29	Papier Mâché II
page	30-32	Self-hardening Clay

Art Edited by Claire Legemah

TWO-CAN

EQUIPMENT I

All the things on these pages have been used somewhere in the MODELS book. You should be able to find them all at home or at school.

Some modelling material is very sticky and hard to get off certain surfaces, so you should always cover the space you are working in and make sure you ask before using things from around the house.

garlic press

fishing twine and wire

pastry cutters

nail brush

cocktail sticks

glue

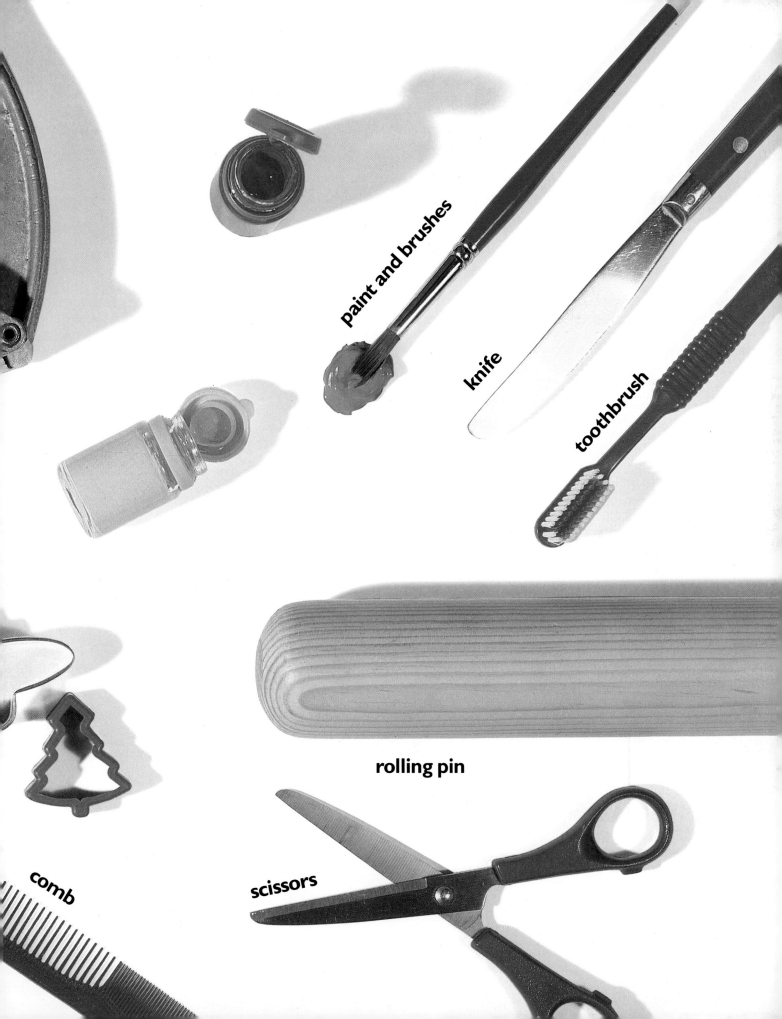

paint and brushes

knife

toothbrush

rolling pin

comb

scissors

Play dough is very easy to make and you can use it again and again. Press it and roll it into shape and add different colours, or decorate your models with other things, like the fishing twine and sequins which make up these fireworks. Play dough is good for moulding too because it spreads to take on the shape of the container it is put in.

Play dough recipe
300g (12 ounces) flour
115g (4 ounces) salt
225 ml (8 fluid ounces) water
2 tablespoons oil
4 tablespoons cream of tartar
food colouring

Mix all the ingredients together and then put them in a saucepan. Ask a grown-up to heat it over a low heat, stirring all the time, until it turns into a ball.

You can use your play dough again and again as long as you store it in a sealed container or a plastic bag.

Make a marzipan teddy bears' picnic! You can buy ready-made marzipan in most large supermarkets. It's great to model with. Just make the basic shapes and fix them together with cocktail sticks.

You can colour the marzipan by kneading in food colouring or by painting it on afterwards. Use fondant icing for fiddly things like bow-ties. Could you make a model of your own teddy?

You can make permanent
decorations like Christmas
ornaments or mobiles with
salt dough.

Dough Recipe

225 g (8 ounces) plain flour
225 g (8 ounces) salt
1 tablespoonful wallpaper paste powder
250 ml (9 fluid ounces) water

Mix the dry ingredients together and then add the water. Roll the dough out to 5 mm (1/4 inch) thickness and then cut out shapes. Make holes in the dough with a cocktail stick so that you can tie ribbons to them when they are dry. Lay on greaseproof paper on a baking sheet and bake for 8 hours in a very cool oven (110°C, 225°F).

When they are cool the models can be painted with poster paints. Allow the paint to dry before adding two coats of varnish. This seals the dough and stops the decorations from going mouldy.

You can make all sorts of amazing badges, buttons and jewellery with oven-baked clay. What about a necklace with all your favourite food?

Clay that you can bake in an ordinary oven is as easy to use as the simplest modelling material.

Roll it out and cut it, or press pieces together gently until they stick. You can use household objects as moulds for your clay. First cover them with baby oil so that the clay doesn't stick when you take it off. Pins and hooks can be added before you bake the clay. Put wire inside narrow parts to make them more secure.

When you bake your models always follow the manufacturer's instructions and ask an adult to help you use the oven. You can varnish your models when they are cool.

Non-hardening clay can be modelled over and over again. There are lots of ways to use it – you can join pieces just by pressing them together. Give the clay a marbled effect by rolling two or three different colours into a ball. Use a nail brush or a garlic press to make lots of different shapes and textures.

You can make almost any model from cake, but it is best to keep the finished shape as simple as possible. First, draw a plan and work out how many pieces of cake you will need and how they will fit together.

Pictures and photographs are useful for inspiration!

Cut the cake to shape and use apricot jam to stick the pieces together. Spread more jam over the cake to help the icing stick.

You can buy ready-made fondant icing for making cake models. Roll out the icing and then drape it over the cake. Fold and cut it into shape. Smooth over any cracks with a little water.

AMO1

Paint the cake with food colouring and decorate it with sweets. You can press some of them into the soft icing but some will need cocktail sticks to keep them in place. Look out for sweets which are the right shape and colour for lights, wheels, or whatever you need for your cake.

Making pottery is easier than you imagine!
  Clay is very cheap and available in most craft shops. If you make mistakes you can always start again.
  Try making a pinch pot by pressing your thumb into a ball of clay and gradually hollowing it out. Or make a coil pot by building up long sausages of clay.
  Remember to keep your clay covered in plastic or a damp cloth when you are not using it or it will dry out.

Make some *slip* from left-over fragments of clay soaked in water. You can use slip to keep the clay you are working on moist and to help stick pieces together. Use an old toothbrush to put the slip on with.

Roll out your clay on a smooth surface and cut out shapes using a knife or cutters.

Make a slab pot by cutting out squares of clay and sticking them to a base. Rub over the joins with lots of slip until they are smooth. You can smooth out your coil pot like this too.

Clay has to be baked in a kiln to make it hard and strong. If you don't have a kiln at school, ask where you can find one in the library or in craft shops.

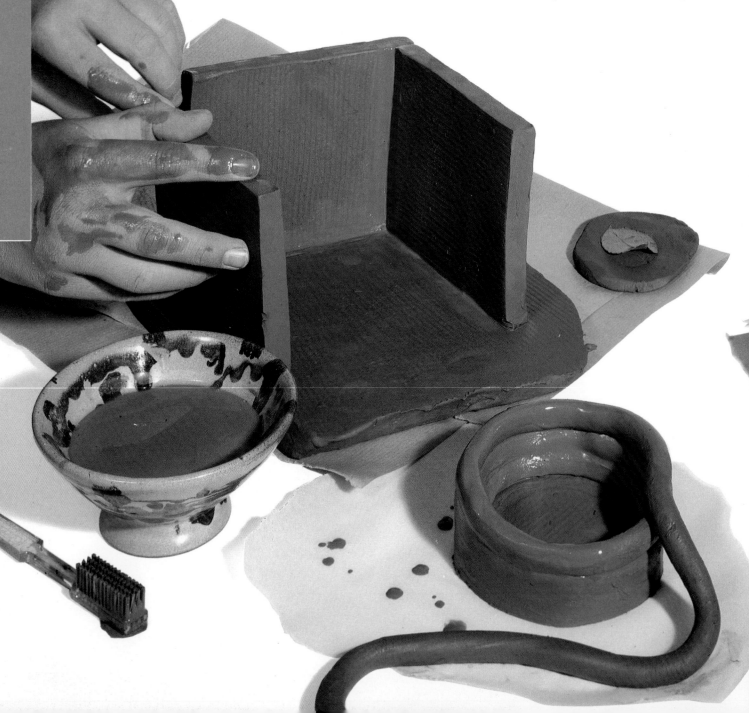

Decorate your pottery when it is still wet by pressing on shapes or making patterns in the clay. When it has been baked you can paint or varnish it.

To make a papier mâché puppet, start off by attaching a balloon to an empty plastic bottle. Secure the neck with a piece of card. Build up six or seven even layers of papier mâché over the balloon until it is firm. When the head is dry, paint the face. Use a piece of garden cane for the arms and make hands by covering pipe-cleaners with papier mâché.

Make a lump of papier mâché for the nose and then fix half a ping-pong ball on top.

To make the clown's costume, you need a rectangular piece of material big enough to cover the bottle. Fold this in half and sew up the sides, leaving a gap for the arms. Cut a hole big enough to slide it over the bottle and then sew it up to the neck. You can cover the join with a bow or a ruffle. Make the hair by cutting equal lengths of wool and attaching them to double-sided sticky tape.

You can make a three-dimensional picture with self-hardening clay. Sketch your picture onto a piece of card and work out what clay shapes you will need to go in it. Make all the pieces separately and allow them to dry. Then paint the pieces and glue them in place on the card. You can mix all sorts of things in with the clay to give different textures.